DREAMTHING

V. Patrick Murolo

And now I'd like to welcome you inward, forward and downward into mad spiral lunacy love...

To: JJ

Odd love or dream thing
No more mumble
Or murmuring

Anytime But A Clock

To inhabit a clock
      Is but for a moment
Hurried and endless and racing and blank
      To beg for atonement
Is not but a moment
      Where time will occupy the reaches of
off
Though on is the war
      So much for the instant
Halted and shadowed and shouting and small
      Though off as we are
And in us is distant
      Just as the minute goes seeking for
more
It is where we dwell
Not a moment to stop
To make love is living
      Just not in a clock

Void There Is No Void There Is No

The arctic vortex of your eyes
Is viral like the space of sun
A cryptic message in the skies
Has let us spiral into one
The lightning white – within your hair
Has filtered through a rip in space
And trickled down within your stare
To match the smile on your face
No matter what – or where you go
You will be worshiped by a dream
And even if the pace is slow
The peace you have will be siren
No matter what – or where you are
Simply you is what will last
And when it rains – or seems too far
Remember
     This void too
       Will pass

If You Want

Every worship felt relieved
Every fire fought through time
Every heart that speeds away
 Is just a way to stay behind
Every sickness stops your peace
All the wreckage you must clean
The jobs of which you give yourself
Must dull the somber thoughts you
dream
Each perception you destroy
Not your fault though maybe mine
I understand if you want to run
I'll look away if you want to cry

Usually Float Around

A slight unsteady
A little shake in the hand
A fearless tremble settled down
A little nervous found a home
A little river cut the wall
To make a mountain proud and tall
A mighty stream
To make them listen
A potent man is born to dream
Usually float around
Somewhere between
A fog and a whisper
Of how things can seem
Of what we can be
Of what mighty words mean
Or how right do they sound
Or if even aloud
To intoxicate crowds
Or to keep what they found
Seldom floating there abound -
In mighty pieces on the ground
And still great walls to go around
And still great walls to go around

The Fall To White

Green tree
Why the gloomy frown
Soon you will be gold and brown
Red and orange in due time
Full and tall and filled with rhyme
As much as one would like to ask
He knows your fountains will not last
Though just before your arches touch
Companions may not notice much
A promise to his giant friend
A wooden shelter till the end
Green tree you are all and right
Stupendous as you fade to white

I'll Go See

Wait here
I'll go see what there is to hear
Fearless unchained into the freezing

Cold for you didn't go with me
Go because you didn't come with me
Blind because you never come see me
Wild because I ran to the animals
Dizzy because you fainted before me
Slight because I want to be careful
Thirsty because I am drinking without you
Weary because I am sleeping alone
Tired because I am chasing a counterfeit
Ailing because I am far beyond sick of it
Weak because I am carrying you
Hungry because I am sharing with you
Faint because I am far from your night
Wait here while I go look for your light
Lock me out only if I let you win
I'll go see nothing if you let me in

Leave It Alone

Stop
And by stop
That means onward and through
Go and by go
That means forward and new
Black
And by black
That means really dark blue
Leave
And by leaving
That means clouds will leave too
An eerie calm placates
Even dry and most unknown
Perhaps the clouds have had enough
Departing silent and alone
The answer stops by quiet
Giving truth to questions known
No one else will ever buy it
For starting over means alone

It Is Now

If ever there was a never will be
It is now
If an everyday lie has ever been lost
It's been found
If a promise is always
It never was there
At last there's a chance
In a fight that's unfair
If ever there was a love to begin
It's not this
If this is the love that you swear
It's amiss
If this is the frozen part
It's become swollen
If this is your healing heart
It must be broken
If ever there was an infinite scene
It's not here
For a distant apologetic dream
It is near
If ever there was another chance
This is how
If never was love to begin

When Destiny Want Us Too

It will happen
We will fracture
We will love
When destiny wants us to
We will
Have laughter and peace
And the dreams of redemption
Our only home is where
She wants it
That is where we are
Warm
And intimate
And broken
And built

As The World Burns Around Me

When all the stars have gone away
And all the suns begin to rise
And all the dreams begin the day
To save perception in your eyes
Another front will face around
And turn you real until you see
That nights before were not so sound
And you were thoughts I'd never be
Although the stars were all still there
I forced my heart to look ahead
And imagined things I could not bear
To force-feed what I never said
When all we are has come to stay
And all the moons have brought us home
A bridge we dreamed of steals the day
And though apart still not alone
So be those daze before sun's fire
And I'll stay thoughts you'd like to be
So be that blaze that is no higher
Please stay the night

Whatsoever

Whatever
With a like for it
Otherwise you'll be without it
You are exactly what you want
Since you know
Since you are the expert
Proficient in what I want
What others whatever's are
Why don't you tell me
What do you want
Anything I have
What waters I run to
Swim out from
Where are you going
I reached out already
I'm waiting
Nevertheless
Now we are equals
Such is like what I am to you -
Whatever

You An All your Maybes

Behind her all the dark minds and dark skies
And there – perched in the foreground is
laughter
Amusement on the whim of knowing
She is winning and she knows it
I have everything but you
You like that – don't you
You want to wrestle with dreams again
So I dive off
I admit defeat
I know it's wrong and a huge mistake
But I want it
You and all your maybes
Look
It was you that I saved
We are so split apart
We are losing and we love it
We are everything but us
I hate that – don't you
You are hard to read and dreaming of me
again
Come down please
You beat me
I submit
I'm begging
I've decided to be your slave

Way More Than Grace

Are the dreams that let you go
For the treasures and wonders are those who catch you
Falling from way more than grace
Those who see what you see in a storm
Those who share the draining disconnect
When you are spent
To surrender
To the grip of love
Is
Arms apart
To captivate
To make prisoner
The storm
Clamp all these hands together
To make captive
To hold souls
Be my judge to keep me safe
Many arms flailing in the past were just waving
Most of them hope with a touch of hurt
Many of them split before their seems were sown
But it's okay
Even the silent electricity of your storm
Keeps me quiet
Even if the dreamless droplets drip from eyes

Every umbrella in your skies stays the same
If you could love me
I would conquer the rain
Every look spliced right with the sky
Makes clouds return white
In the blink of an eye
Even in the blinking
There will be daze that sink your dream
Even in the sinking there will be words you
want to leave
Even if those words in anger
Come to halt a fellow voice
There will come a hollow fork
 Even still without a choice
Even if you choose to think
There will be those who wish to stop it
Even if you come with courage
You will be told to swiftly drop it
Even on daze you speak the truth
There will be words you were not thinking
But even in the grief of thought
Is clearly end and then beginning
Even if you promise
Even if you leave
All you have to do is blink
But you will still believe
That even if you're sad

And no one cares
And no one knows
Less are those it takes to catch
But more than grace to let you go

It's Jokes About

All the elsewhere's
Speeding
Leaving
Thinking racing
Is good and
Trusting
And nevertheless
Loves you
More when
You're sleeping
Not when you're speaking
Every where else
Greedy
Eating everything
Bested
Here with hearts
You had so much
Invested
Not rested
But tyrants
And lusting
For elsewhere
For new misfits
For their abundance
It's jokes about
It's gunna be okay
Nevertheless loves you

You Have Me

Don't be alive
Anymore
She cried
Damn it don't be broken
Touch the future
You can't get it
The wind blows both ways baby
You don't have me

DreamThing

My thing my dream.
Had gone away it seemed
Like bolts from a heaven
Somewhere far or in between
All the thoughts from all the day
Always go the other way
The things I think my dreams will be
Were never real and always leave
They always go their own way home
Unlike things I thought I had known
And every image I create
Would turn reverse and then escape
But back they always come with fury
And back they always come to burn
They lack the colors of my worry
My thing my dream has so returned
More than any other
In the whole wide beginning
More than any summer that's been gone for
years
More than the globe may be off and on
spinning
More than where ghosts have been spending
their tears
Always off and on again wanting
The past of our ghosts
Always

Back again haunting
I know you wont believe me so
I see you want our thing to go
It's crazy how the tide has turned
Somewhere far from what I've learned
An answer shows itself in debt
Though do not ask my dream to start
And though your word is what I get
My thing
My dream
Is not your heart

People Sometimes Do Things

In the hush of the mornings middle maze
There drips around a golden web
Not forgone – a plague without
People do things in their head
And people sometimes do things wrong
One day they will live instead

To Quit It

It's getting really
Really profound
Around here
Kind of heavy sorry eyes
Sorry about that
Shouldn't grovel
It's getting deep in here sometimes
It's getting really
Really hard
To see around here
Kind of almost blind
Don't get upset
Apology accepted
It's just really hard to rewind
This time it's very
Very important
About how
Kind of almost gone
It could have gotten
It's nobodies fault
It's just really hard to go back right now
It just kind of
Happened that way back then
Right now
Tomorrow and the ego
And the next time
And again and again and again

It could have been over
It's kind of going that way
Last time
Don't be sorry
It either will not
Or will withstand
It's just really tough to pick a day
For once in your life
There is love there
If you take it
It's waiting
There by the war
If you make it
Great oceans
If you drift
And false conquests
If you don't admit it
The truth –
That's a funny forest
That simply withers
And laughs
As it goes
For your rift
That you split
When
you seem uncertain
for now its unbearable
it's just really hard to rewind right now

You're A Good Snake

Off to blend in again
You are my favorite snake
And well equipped to hide in the scene
Always an opportunist –
You'll eat the exposed or anything
You may be in the trees watching
Or dug in desert tans
To strike at any shadow forest
Or heat seekers in the sand
So agile
You are very good at wrapping around
God's candy
Or fruit
My very best sidewinder
Coils fantastic in a loop
You prefer us dead
But you'll eat the live
I think
Well maybe not
You'll know I'm alive
When the fruit starts to rot

Negative Dream

Negative space
Is good to be
A negative face
Or a negative tree
A secret race
Is going
Is on
A negative place
Is good and gone
Your negative lips
A volatile sweet
A negative gloss
An infinite treat
The negative spaces
You lean between
Far - and all it was worth
Was a negative dream

Who's Mind Is Yours

Her mind is always
Chattering
Always chattering
Always chill
Always and forever
Throwing fits
In my mind
Always will
All these games I love to hate
All these wars I love to play
Maybe we are soul mates – on these floors
I'll give you money if you stay
Now to take it
Now too far
Now to take my mind away

A Soul In My Fire

An impulse in my laughter
A motive for inviting
A vast mood moving faster
 Tricks my life to think I'm dieing
Aware I am
No less or knowing
Forced to keep on hurt
And growing
Made to crumble
To tolerate
There is water everywhere
Damage much like cyclones grieve
There was damage anyway
Much more than the cyclones leave
A fire on soul
Means only more flames to acquire
Or that which the devastation begs for in
desire
To prove I am aware
And that you are also a liar
I will open and show you
A soul in my fire

Pretty One

Don't be that weary
There's a lot you didn't want to know
Don't be so crazy
Scary in the worlds you go
No one will believe what you mean
If you insist to keep preaching beyond what
you've seen
Or agree with your beauty
Or lean where you lean
You could get away
With breaking anyone into anywhere
And take anything
Don't be that dream
No one suspects the...

All The Eyelids

All the eyelids ever do
Is leave and never come back through
Passing until the other side
In hopes to return shut in time
Departed in the wile of games
In hopes to see them open again
All the eyelids care is color
Though some sporadic like no other
Gaining until the passage of help
Shows eyelid more than the eye itself

What I Wanted To Tell You Tomorrow

If you think your future is there
I want you to stay
If you think your future is here
Then go
I would beg
Though courage is in short supply
I would hold
Though my grip is too strong
I would weep
But it's just too sad
I would say thank you
But I am too sorry
Except for all the laughing
I would say this is funny
Tomorrow would have been perfect to say this
But I'd rather ruin the moment now
Well the offer is always there

See Us

See us being holy together
Do you have eyes on your hands
No
 But you do have them in the back of your
head
Do you have reservations
Like forever about always
See us being caught together
Revolution against required ticking clocks
See us virus in your eyes
See us being with a possible

Shapes

And stones
Amid condensations
To draw upon
To write cruel jokes
Funny antics
Or I love love love you
I'd rather it be no than nothing at all
Come back as anything
Just tell me what's in the amazing heart thing
you have
That generous giving vessel of all that's ever
been
Was – is now – the way you are beautiful
always was
And always will be
I've seen the way they look at you
A face – that which could make a man give up
His holy convictions
Spirit – all beliefs
His predetermined beliefs in Gods and ghosts
And old old stories – your face kills faith
Your heart creates hunger
Your smile melts away all the burning monks
You rebalance the off of all –
You are why we paint on the silence of walls
You are why I still look for shapes
In the very vast wastelands of being awake

Not Like Them

I'm sorry this changes everything
I'm sorry for what I turned out to be
Just another gigantic fool
Maybe I'll get what I want and the wrong thing
But if I think twice
Maybe I want and will get something better
There is nothing better
I have to sleep now
I've poisoned myself
To teach reality a lesson
I'll show them
I'll show them all
I love love love you
Remember who does
And who just wants to use you up
Don't put me in the same sort as them
I'm not sorry I set myself apart

See What You Do

A light a pain a world and such
A light a pain I touch too much
See what you are
You're the pain and the pills and the world
And a crutch
A muse I used to feel used and abused
It had to really hurt
The bigger the wound
The more you loved me
The better it feels when you leave
See what you do
I hurt alone through no fault of your own
You're insane and my hills and the world
To me I can live and be
The better I'll heal when you cut me free

Tell Me You

Since you wont voice it or show me
I turned to something physical
Something to touch
To project what you are feeling in your mind
Thinking in your heart
Let me know
Tell me when you're ready ok

Put It Away

It's time to put it away now see
The past has merged with guilt and me
It's time to put it away now you
All the love has fused with dreams of truth
Go on without us
Without illusions or trust
Push us deep as you can
Down past in love again
To you it feels right
I have no more to say
You think it's time
      I put you away

Too Many Millions Of Miles To Go

Waiting and fading
For space and for stars
Thinking how many millions of miles you are
Silly things could be
If this were for real
So far from the sun makes it too hard to feel
If this were not could have been
It might be a game
So within touch that it might be again
So what of this traveler
Too many long trips
The heart is just fine while the mind remains
sick
Tricks you have uncovered
Doubts you never reveal
The meantime is enough for you
And all that which you feel
This is not real
To much time blown
How many more millions of miles my love
Do you wish for me to go

We Have A thing

Defensive like a gun
Don't leave
Deadly like a shield
Just go
Just when I thought you were into warring with
me
You woke up with dawn at your feet
And stood staring majestic into the horizon
Somehow the scope of all things grew larger
And you left
And me behind missing the boat again of
course
Sailing away without a scribe
Someone that could have come and painted
you
With the colors of whatever fit
Beneath stars that lifted low into the silent
thing
The dreamy damaged nights we wasted
Remember

I'm sorry

You're Like A Million Miles Away

What is it
You're like a million miles away
Do you need anything
Are you hurt
I have something very important to tell you
But it's too important to shout
From a distance
Tell
Your drift is making me smile and crazy
Are you mad
At me
I just wanted to send my love
The heart-stop pain is made of steel
Trust was this
And a friend of mine
Me too but
Your backlash is like
Me too but
 I want more
Me
Too
But I like when you say
Things like that to me
Too but
Sorry I've been all distant
It's ok
You haven't been

You don't owe me
Every single thing
Just wanted to say hi and
 Send my love no matter

 What is it
You're like...

Tomorrow Tonight

Tonight
Caught in
The middle of this little town
We will be looking
For something else
Besides each other
Together close to nowhere
With luck and religion
We might just
Be lifted
And let go of what's
Been going on
A tiny world on a cliff
In our hands
The choice to let go
Or pull back from the brink
And continue on
With the ride of the millennium
Thrust us
Mysterious
Into tomorrow - tonight

Inviting Nightmares

I too invite nightmares into my light
Whatever you are willing to die for – give it up
Live by what you stand for
Stand for what you live by
Be careful of what you'd die for
It might die with you
Anything you are willing to die for
Dies quickly
Most of us – arrogance

Is The Love Oasis

Out through the sun and over her hills
Not for the milk that my love has spilled
If not for the people that make me feel bold
My love the oasis would not be so cold
But I told the sun all he needed to know
It was I that killed gardens
Nonesuch to protests
It was I that cast snow
It was I who felt blessed
Though out there with others I made me alone
I never went for where gardens have grown
And out here are people that I feel inside
Have no way of knowing where I've tried to
hide
But my love oasis has nothing to say
 admit some relief when she walks away
Though not to defeat the great purpose we
made
I'm sorry the price my heart forced her to pay
I love you and will not obey random hearts
So alive and such freedom when she is apart
I won't leave you behind even after you go
Tonight tells me everything I needed to know

Dreamthing

Sometimes I stand on Great hills and sink
Sometimes I need to stand up to think
I stood with heel marks on my shoulders and
lived
All the while I sat between wars that we did
Conflicting with time-bombs set to set free
All that was searching without thirsting for me
I want no more war
Between me you and the rest
Both ways make me love
So much more than what was left
I'll bet – if you dream a thing like what you
are
And what you will always be
A dream thing much more certain thinks
Of all the things we mean
To the world and her - each other's measure
A test to all that features pleasure
A waste to keep going
Or not to be heard
You know what it's like
To bleed the absurd
Though now I believe it's too short not to trust
I have no choice but to seek truth
In this muck
And make do with whatever dream things
Have spoken

Have gone
The only scar here is broken
And long
Not on my knees
Nor my soul within reach
The world – rising away
Has a dream thing for each

You Creature You

Just like the creature
She moves
Remember
She was like fluid
Pretender
Like she loves
She is movement
And just like the creature
She reaches out
In sleepless creature night creeps
Creeping like a cold blooded
Reptilian relic of loves past
Lost
Lingering

Stay Brave And Awake

I know you're tired
I know you're afraid
We are both too wired
To fix what we made
To find in a distant fire
A better night and instant daze
Your resistance has been willful and brave
To fend off and mend with me
The messes we made
I love you – no lie
You keep me just frayed
I'd wish you goodbye
If only you'd stay
I've got a few more walls to cross
You can come if you want
I'll be good to you
And strong for you
I'm sorry for all I forgot
You distract me from you
I wont be flawless
But I'm yours without fear
Actually I'm always afraid
I think everyone is in a way
I'll love you – no lie

Only The Glue

So what
If it's true
It tastes good when it's new
Don't play who me
With games that don't stick
Don't play with glue
If it's true it's a trick
So what now
If it's true
It hurts hard
Where to go
Too much to do
How many answers to know
Don't say it's new
When it's not even old

When She Is Herself

Wrong
In the presence of
When she is sober
She is the most charming
Long
In the pleasance of
When she is horrible
She is mostly herself

Out Cold

Layer upon layer
Stratum below stratum
Peeled back for fun
To be fair
It was gruesome
There - but not really
Too absent to see
Look again stranger
No more monster to be
Live again low enough
Out cold in scary dreams
Out there alone we love
We are more together than it seems
For when we turn over
And take back the warm we dare
We peel back and in wonder
Find there's not much else in there

Say It With

Whoever you are
Whatever your love is
Will you with the wind crumble
Quick at the sight of adore
Resistant in the face of mirrors
Beloved in the race and race for
Be downward and enlightened
With the right you are a fraud
With the truth you are afraid
Of this and all that ever was
For bliss and your sick take on love
For rain and when you ever shine
For we and all our words are blind
So say it through the voice of time

She Thinks She Is

Almost
And wonderful
Broke down
Better than heavens
Built up better than hell
There are things she would change
But knows she is perfect
Pure
Flawed
Pristine
And damaged

The Volatile

The volatile and
The subservient one
Both in the same
Still curious fun
Yes is little temper fate
Yes it can and detonates
No bomb bursts better
No more empty awaits
Then when this little temper
Fixes up to escape

And Discover

Here on everlasting seas
The ocean of a stormy peace
A calm of what we lost to speed
And insults that we really mean
I exalt
I at fault
I the thief
I the lover
We only mean half of what we say
And discover

Else

The cool sun has almost risen
And a strange plane goes diagonal
Slow motion medium speed
Descending to somewhere else
Not here
not earth
and elsewhere through the cutting of time
and water
a sad silly time – it's still
an existence - it's just somewhere else
fabricated with the wishes
of those who can fly
stuck here
we must do this
and then that
and then give up our ghost
To Whom
To what
To where did you wish to land
My love and my only beast
What happened to your only head
It's lost and you're not looking
Don't give up before the ghost
Don't pretend to fly
Don't predict such heavenly things
Stop protecting phony wings
To this

To that
To most degrees of the coming sun
Where do you think you are
To whom are you going to tell
We always believe there's something better
Something higher
Something else

You know I know

This Is What You Wanted

Yeah when I get mad I give
But you are always always taken
It's not that you are wholly mine
But god this thing is so forsaken
No when I don't freak you love
But this is not to far from theft
What's the lie in which you seek
I am all but out of breath
One breath left to figure out
One breath left to go without
Stab one breath with eyes of stone
Piercing through the thoughts we've known
Happy words are so untrue
They take from me and give to you
All that you wanted was both our eyes closing
Both of us leaping - neither of us knowing

With This

There was a week or two
Where we didn't dream
We gazed stoned at the great summer skies
Are we leaving with them
Are you ok with that
Are we again
Excuses we missed
Are you happy with that
Are you happy

For Love To Love Of Love

Await
What with want
Wanted waiting
Awake
And with what
Wanted nothing
Asleep
But with dreams
Haunted heaven
Alert
When with want
Came the anything
Aware
But with that
Waited no one

No One Else Has Yours

For the depth of your heart
For the good of your soul
For the daze that are chaos
And nights in control
For the meager horizon
In which you have faith
And the orbit set back
To complete your escape
For the hoods that you where
And the masks you will steal
For those you have dared
To convince they can feel
No one could fall better
Than you yourself
Or your beliefs
No one strung so many lies
Or sought emotions that you've reached

The Sun Is Out

Peeking in and
Out
The sun lit sky
    Looks free
Touching the cloud
    Lines
Are just
The tips
Of the hollow tree
The sun lit day
Is yellow
    For you
But gray
For me
Some
Will say
For shame on me
To put that shame
On some
Impossible
Thing
I will

Tell from the treetops
Put
That
Blame
Where it belongs
Alone
With some responsible
Dream

Really Very

Always
Always
Always taking
Always faking real escaping
Always making me
Feel stupid
The insect ate it
The people bought it
We can meet outside the church
If you want it
Not to worry
Far and plain
You have humbled quite the tame
Along with fields of purple wheat
All your perfect
Gods are neat
I mean
I'm very black about your hair
Really dark about your eyes
On the fence about your skin
Kind of sick of your disguise
But fragments of a better spring
Of all the seasons – this one brings
Fragments of a warmer day

Often calm and muted quiet
The creepy sky
Is well within itself a riot
A hell above us
Large and silent
I'm sorry to see you so
In control
We all know I gave that up
A long time ago
So for forever
What and when we are
Forever and the dust of stars
Always we are thus departed

Really You Want More

Too many traps
An overabundance of ways
You fox
So many steps
A mighty way you trick
You hoax
A million victories
And you want more
Here -

The Super Pretender

All hail the super pretender
The likes of which I'll never remember
All allegiance to the pretty suspender
Hovering
I can't believe it snowed last night
Like all my fears
It came down
Tumbling
Far into spring
Likewise while I'm here
I can't believe I'm yelling
Too far I think
Maybe too much
In the many edges of fear
Mostly one

Our Dream One

Share my dreams where I am late
I know you share them on your own
Now show me where you fell asleep
To join me in duress and dream
We both fall short – in every slumber
And think it's real – to overcome
A massive action – though we try
Our bad dream comes apart
As one

We Cut What We Are

Hope you are well
And not too far
Gone like the ways
That you were like
Before when we loved
And still my heart
Beating goes on
Gone like you are
Happy without bliss
And happy within
This is the name of
The game that we named
For you to forget
For nothings the same
As it was when we loved
When we sunk each of
Ours and all we ignited
Together in lightning
And storms
It is righted we were
This and naïve
And all you gave up
Was what you believed
And the ties that we cut

Instead

You wanted perfect
But you got me
Sorry bout that
I thought I could take the whipping
But I cant
You wanted a nobody
But you got me
Sorry bout that
I thought I could push myself aside
But I cant
You wanted a free man
But instead you got a slave
Sorry bout that
I am a servant
Even for you I will not change

That Red Velvet Voice Of Hers

That red velvet voice of hers
Makes even the best seer blind
That red velvet voice she has
Makes even visions out of time
That deep raspberry thing
Booming quiet loud and soft
A sound unlike what others dream
It works in peace and wars she fought
That steep and sudden pause awakes
No matter what or who she makes
These things- that voice that you create
Sound like visions seeking no escape
It's something I've never heard before
Some sort of humming I can't ignore
What is your voice – but a vision in a door
 Makes even the best sounding dreamers
 Regret they hadn't listened more

Hard To Know

To live to be to know you exist
That and that is the most war
The hardest most for
The most of what
What can I do more
Who else should I give
Why else would I be
To live
To think you're alive
To know you exist
Its hard

Totally Intentional

I didn't mean to spit on those flowers
Sorry I purposely wasted those hours
I didn't know it would cause all of this
Sorry for guessing that we would go sour
I didn't mean to seem so disturbed
If I had known that your dream was to never
be burned
I would have been less for you –
I would have told you I heard
For what was absurd was the best that we
were
You should have told me you weren't ready

Opaque

In the remainder of the morning trees
There is a life of love of love
And in the sharp distance cries a breeze
Waiting for wings to raise her above
Everyone wants to go away
Everything parting chooses it's day
Don't be sad about us -
You are not lost – you were left here
Unless you can trust
It's not love against fear
You will not shed the dust
You will never appear

Can I Have Some Me Please

I have enough for one more
Its not another -
Do you have more for me
Is it -
Do you -
Have any more of me left in there
  Please - I need some

The Water From

They - born to live
They die on their feet
See lovers whimper
Be love or defeat
He – all but born again
She baptizes with lips
The waters soft has never been
Whatever comes from this new trip
Does this child have the right
And would it be too hard to give
Such a flame a torching light
Whatever happens we shall live
Whatever happens we may fight
Wherever we go now we will beg
We burned our eyes and found our head
Whatever happens we have this
The water from our searing lips

I'm Not Sorry

I'm sorry I don't believe you
But I can't
Sorry I have to leave you
But I won't
Sorry I want you back
But I don't
Sorry I cannot save you
But I will
Sorry I didn't trust you
But I did
Sorry I tried to be alive
But I am

Aftertaste

Look at he who is wasting you and your pretty
little face
Look up at me
When you're doing that
Give to him some glossy almond taste
Is it he who gives you so much treasure
And the pleasure you so craved
Was it worth it when you trampled all that I
had tried to save
Hold there at home where I once drank upon
your
Waist
And settle on a lesser thing to keep tempo
with your race
Look there at me watching - he who simply
always tastes
The salty bitter flavor of your pretty little face

And Walk At The Same Time

Hereafter long lingering
Summer insects fluttering
In perfect landscapes and uttering
You my botany are sublime
We cannot want and walk at the same time
You picked your devils
And showed them your favorite wilderness
Everything I picked is leveled
My true Devil is oppressed
Please don't go out now
For near is the sun
And close is the high
Come back soon into this garden
I'll be there to meet you outside
Now is the place
And here is the time
I confess to a memory
That you were sublime
And if tragic – we will handle
And if magic – we will cope
If it's epic – we can make it
However vast it seems to scope

I'll never tell you no again

Let me take this trip with you
If memory is there to just remind
We are forever on the same path
But never at the same time

A Someday You

I think in freedom
You believe in yourself
I think in the cave
You won't take my help
I think in respect
You lack the skill
But when you bear another son of god
Mother of mercy – I think you will
Force a ton to rethink its weight
I know it's a lot to hold on your shoulder
Your slouching oppression is quiet and down
I'll trade you your honesty for my resolve
May I mention it – or is that not allowed
Watch out there little thing
Look out there where sundown meets the
brittle wing
If in the great blue scene here between
Is so sweet – is so close
And is still there alive
It's won't be because oblivion lied
Rather all the infinite treats
I'm so happy I could howl
Here at the moon or whatever you have
Giving the earth what she's never had
You think that's a delusion

That I cannot kill
You are the solution
And one day I will

Go Dawn Go

Go dawn go
Reach and be bold
Arrive to where horizons fold
Surf down from the sky
Or like soft wings fly
Flutter and float fantastically all you want
I'll be there when you crash

A Change In Life On Earth For

Relax
And take a hint
With me
A chance for a forever we
A change in life on earth for us
A bitter end to squall that was
A gritty start was ours to have
And now there is a chance to grab
This change on earth in life for sure
Whatever love was ever worth
A place to pick intrepid sands
With two misguided newborn hands
This only open space is free
And endless dreams allotted we
A mind aware of never was
Is more alike the lines of love
For first and foremost where we grow
In the boundary we cannot shut
This the shapes of where we go
A change in life on earth for
What

Years We Have

Not a part of yesterday
A story not unlike was ours
To have to make to love to play
Unattached in fallen years
Ours was ours to have today
But late to come and so unclear
And so apart from home the world
And so depart from all you feel
And go into that place of yours
To fall apart from years and years
We had we made we loved we played
And went the way we thought was real
It's not a waste of now and here
But fate begins to fade and clear
Truly with our souls we paid
And with our thoughts too far from near
We stand apart from our tomorrow
And will not end to be enslaved
A love so not apart to follow
Within my heart for years and years

But My Light Love

Where did you go
When you took me away from here
But my light love
What did you find when you found me in there

But my light love always stays so far from near
I don't intend to stray too far from the shore
But my light love is a notion
That the ocean must ignore
But my light love was an answer
To a love I didn't intend
 So by love light
And by birth rite
I am doomed to love again –

But my light love
Was the bright ever real to begin
What is right love
Was it worthy to feel – worthy of sin
And at night love
The only light is fake and freezing
Can't we just pretend for now
That there is something like a beacon
Not above – but far and out

Beyond this ocean of our own doubt
But my light love
Like the day
Must see us through to the bitter end
With all these love lights and tomorrows
We are doomed to love again

The End

An eternal thank you to Mike, Liz, Dominic and Sarah for your unending inspiration and support....

V...

?

When you're reaching up - still too short
And speaking up but still ignored
If you're too excited to be bored
You're moving slow but thinking fast
Always first in line to finish last
If you study truth and learn a lie
If you look for proof in places you hide
You may think you are fractured
But your heart is in tact
This love will recapture
Your sun will come back

In through the trees and out through the wind
Out through the outer places space would begin
Look past the stars today
Tonight you will know

Love always,

Your *V*

www.ingramcontent.com/pod-product-compliance
Lightning Source LLC
Chambersburg PA
CBHW070831180526
45168CB00002B/803